613.25
Sanc

Over-eating, let's talk about it

Overeating

Lets talk about it

Overeating

Let's Talk About It

by Gail Jones Sanchez
and Mary Gerbino

Illustrated by Lucy Miskiewicz

Dillon Press, Inc., Minneapolis, Minnesota 55415

Dedications

I wish to dedicate this book to children. May your days be filled with sunshine, and your plates with wholesome, tasty food, in quantities large enough to satisfy your hunger, but not so large as to burden your body.

M.G.

I dedicate this book to Cynthia Martinez, Joni Gayle George, and Hazel Jones George.

G.J.S.

Library of Congress Cataloging in Publication Data

Sanchez, Gail Jones.
   Overeating : let's talk about it.

   Includes index.
   Summary: Examines the reasons and the consequences of being overweight, and offers advice on changing one's eating habits for the better.
   1. Obesity in children—Juvenile literature. 2. Children—Nutrition—Juvenile literature. [1. Obesity. 2. Weight control. 3. Diet] I. Gerbino, Mary. II. Title.
RJ399.C6S26   1986   616.3'98   85-25388
ISBN 0-87518-319-0

Dillon Press, Inc., 242 Portland Avenue South
Minneapolis, Minnesota 55415

Printed in the United States of America
1 2 3 4 5 6 7 8 9 10 95 94 93 92 91 90 89 88 87 86

Acknowledgments

To those who helped us with suggestions and encouragement, we extend our appreciation.

Foremost is Diana Colby, Children's Librarian for the Santa Clara County Library System. A talented, generous woman, Colby shared her vast knowledge of children and their reading preferences with us. Others read and reread our manuscript, and helped us know our readers and their needs. Among those are Carol Begley, Mary Buxton, Dorothy Davis, Cynthia Martinez, Pat McAndrews, Alyce McManus, Orpha Quadros, and Helen Williams; we thank them for their time and ideas.

A special thank you to the Tuesday Night Meeting of Overeaters Anonymous, in Fremont, California. We wish them success.

Contents

Part I

Knowing the Reasons

You may need to work on feeling good about yourself before you can take charge of your eating.

CHAPTER 1

Why Do People Overeat?

The main topic of this book is NOT diets or calorie charts or low-fat menus.

Over the long run, reducing diets do not work. People who lose weight by crash dieting gain it back quickly, and afterward feel more frustrated than ever. It is also possible that crash dieters can damage their health with their diets.

The main topic of this book is overeating: why people do it, and what can be done to stop it. People young and old overeat for many reasons. If you are overweight, it is important to learn the reasons in your life that led to your overeating habits. When you learn the reasons, you can then deal with the problem.

For a start, we'll tell you about some of the young people we know.

• Angie is a quiet rebel. She eats when she's angry with her parents. They find fault with the way she looks and the things she does. Her mother says soon they will have to buy her clothes from a tentmaker. Her father says the only time she moves is to go to the ice cream shop. Angie was taught that it's not nice to be angry at her parents, so she swallows her anger with great amounts of food. Most of the time she sneaks the food, because her parents criticize her for snacking, too.

• When Kevin comes home from school, he is alone for four hours until his parents return from work. He gets tired of television and computer games. Kevin wants to talk to someone, but no one is there. So instead, he mixes up and bakes brownies. He doesn't tell his parents how scared he feels in the house alone. They would think he was a baby. He eats to fight the boredom and the fear.

• Jared's parents are divorced. Since the divorce, he doesn't see his father very much, because his father travels and can visit Jared only once a month. When Jared starts to miss his father, all the way to his toes, he eats a big bag of potato chips, because that's what he and his dad used to eat while they did his homework. He washes the chips down with sodas. When he sees his father, Jared doesn't want to complain about things; he wants to have a good time. On the other hand, Jared can't tell his mother how much he misses his father; that makes her unhappy, and Jared loves both his parents. He tries to eat his way out of this trap.

• Mary Jane hates the way her classmates treat her at school; she thinks it's because of the way she looks. They call her Tubbs and Fatso and The Queen Mary. When popular kids choose up sides for games, Mary Jane is left out. She says her round body is the reason they don't include her. Mary Jane feels depressed and sad, so she eats more snacks to ease the pain.

• In Andy's house, everyone is busy. No one seems to have time for him. His big sister is always on the phone talking to her boyfriend. Volunteer work for the church takes up most of his mother's time. His father works second shift at the auto plant and is gone during the evening. Andy's house is in an older neighborhood, and there are no kids his age to play with. He feels that no one loves him or has time for him. When he eats plates full of the cookies and cupcakes his mother bakes, he feels he has a part of her.

You may be able to think of other ways people use overeating to fill the gaps in their lives.

Being overweight most often comes down to your feelings about yourself. Officially, that's called self-esteem. If your self-esteem is low—that is, if you feel you're not pretty or handsome or clever or smart or important enough to make it in your social world of school and family—you may fill in the gap (and your waistline) with high-calorie snacks. You are caught on the never-ending "fat wheel." One of the first steps in ending overeating is to take a look at your self-esteem. You may need to work on feeling good about yourself before you can take charge of your eating.

Many young people feel a lot of pressure. They think they have no choices and can't do anything to change the situations that make them unhappy. In a lot of homes, for example, parents must work away from the house all day. That leaves young people to find their own recreation. Some of these people begin to use eating as a cure for loneliness, as a way to pass the time, or just as something to do while they are waiting for their parents to return. Being alone is a pressure for young people.

Some young people use food as a way to get even with those who find fault with them. They eat most of their food when no one is looking. In their upside-down way of thinking, they get revenge on

WHEEL OF NEVER-ENDING FAT

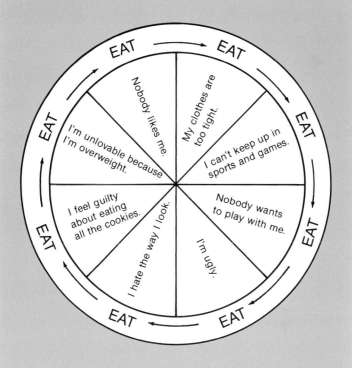

Do you have a never-ending list
of reasons to keep eating?

those who criticize them for being overweight by
eating more. Criticism is another pressure.

All of the people we've discussed in this chapter have pressure, too. But they all can work on

these situations by speaking honestly about the feelings they have. If they never say anything about problems, the chances are good that the problems will not be solved. And if these people don't put themselves in charge of their own eating habits, they will continue to be overweight.

Families and family situations aren't the only source of pressure on boys and girls. The whole world seems to contain very different messages about eating and about being overweight. For example, food companies produce millions of dollars worth of foods that taste sweet or salty or chocolaty or spicy. Then, the companies spend even more money on television and magazine ads to convince people that these foods are terrific. Through advertising, they suggest that life will be more fun when you eat these foods. What they don't tell you is that these foods don't contribute much of anything except calories to a person's body.

The same body that's supposed to absorb countless snacks is also supposed to be thin. Billboards, magazines, newspapers, and television all show thin people having fun. We're all supposed to look like them in order to have fun like them When overweight people are shown on television, they're sometimes shown as clumsy, cartoon people, or else as villains. If you stop to think about it, though, being fat has little to do with being clumsy or evil, and being thin doesn't mean you'll always have a good time.

In North America, many people are too concerned about their weight. Some people even diet when there is no need. If you think you are overweight, take a good look at your body. The mirror is a better check than a scale.

Do you have bulges around your middle that your normal-weight friends do not have? Have you checked with your doctor or the school nurse to see what you should weigh for your age and height? In this chapter we have included a chart that has the best information on "normal" weights that we could find. Even so, not every list of numbers applies to every person. The chart is only a guide. Generally, people are considered to be overweight if they are thirty percent more than normal. That is, if you weigh ninety-eight pounds, and the chart says you should weight seventy-six pounds, then you are thirty percent overweight for your age and height.

If you are overweight, you probably can think of quite a few reasons for dropping your extra pounds. You might want to be better at sports. You may want the kinds of clothes that thinner

Weight Chart for Boys

Age	Average Height	Average Weight	Overweight
8	50"	60 lb.	78+ lb.
9	53"	64 lb. (54-74 lb.)	84+ lb.
10	55"	68 lb.	88+ lb.
11	57"	76 lb. (65-87 lb.)	98+ lb.
12	59"	90 lb.	117+ lb.
13	61"	94 lb. (80-108 lb.)	124+ lb.

This weight chart is only a guide. Extra numbers under ages 9, 11, and 13 show how average weights can vary because of growth spurts. Your normal weight might vary 10 pounds more or less than the average weights shown

people wear. Maybe you want more people to admire the way you look. Perhaps people wouldn't give you such a hard time if you were thinner.

Besides social and mental reasons, there are health reasons for losing weight as well. Bodies that are overweight for many years become less and less healthy. They are more likely to experience serious illnesses such as heart disease and diabetes. By being careful about your weight at every age, you stand a better chance at good health throughout your life.

Weight Chart for Girls

Age	Average Height	Average Weight	Overweight
8	49"	55 lb.	71+ lb.
9	52"	62 lb. (58-67 lb.)	80+ lb.
10	54"	67 lb.	87+ lb.
11	56"	76 lb. (68-84 lb.)	98+ lb.
12	58"	92 lb.	120+ lb.
13	61"	98 lb. (91-107 lb.)	128+ lb.

as you grow taller. But, if your weight passes the number in the overweight column, you should examine your eating habits. You are probably overweight.

Once you have looked at your body and your weight, you'll know if it's time to take control of your eating. Now, how do you do it? In the chapters ahead we'll look at some ways of thinking that help keep a person overeating and unhappy about it. We'll suggest new ways of thinking and behaving that can help you control your eating. Later, we'll offer some practical advice on foods and activities that can help you toward your goal of losing extra weight.

Keeping weight off forever begins with the self-esteem you have.

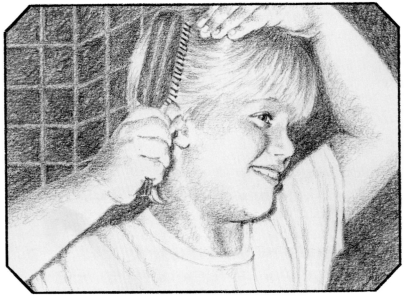

You have to work at liking yourself.

CHAPTER 2

Attitudes—the Choice Is Yours!

Let's suppose you have checked the mirror for bulges on your body, looked at the weight chart, and found that you are in the overweight column. Now, you want to do something about that. Before you can change your appearance, you will have to work on your attitude about yourself.

Try this Quickie Quiz.

1. Do you hate going shopping for clothes?
2. Do you say mean things about yourself, such as "I'm too fat to look good in anything" or "I'm ugly"?
3. Do you often feel angry with yourself?
4. Do you refuse to go swimming, to the beach, or on a picnic because you don't have anything to wear that fits you, or don't want to be seen in what you have—swimsuit, shorts, and so on?

If you answer yes to these questions, you are being too hard on yourself. If others say these things about you, they are also being too critical.

You must start by saying, "I do not look ugly now, AND I will look better when my body is a normal size."

Begin with these steps:

1. Become aware of the negative thoughts you are thinking.
2. When you hear critical thoughts in your mind, stop them.
3. Replace each critical thought with a good one about yourself.

This takes some practice, but you can do it if you keep at it. Here are some examples of good thoughts you can use for a beginning:

- *I am a special person—there is no one in the whole world exactly like me.*

- *I am lovable.*

- *People will want to have me at their parties because I am nice to others.*

- *I am a good friend.*

- *I am in control of my own life. I get up in*

the morning by myself. I care for my personal hygiene. I do my chores. I can walk past the refrigerator without stopping to taste the food inside.

- *I am honest.*

- *Although it will be very hard to undo my overeating habits, I can do it, because I want to.*

- *I must change my negative thinking. I can say I did a clumsy thing without saying I am clumsy.*

- *When people say critical things about my appearance, I will not allow their words to become part of my own thinking about myself.*

You have to work at liking yourself. It's something only you can do for yourself.

Everyone does many things that he or she can be proud of. Make a list of your good points. Do you take good care of your pets? Do you have chores that always get done? Are you good at math or spelling or gardening or woodworking or sewing? Do you run errands for your parents or neighbors? Are you good at memorizing things? Do you play an instrument or sing well?

You may have said no to each of the above questions. That doesn't matter. Remember, everyone is different, and everyone is a special combination of good points. In making up your own list, think of the times you feel good about yourself and what you're doing. Having negative thoughts about yourself is, in part, a habit. If you can learn to say to yourself, "Hey, that was good!" when you deserve it, you can pick up a new habit—positive thinking.

Changing any habit is one of the toughest things anyone can do. It means fighting against doing things the same old way just because you're used to them. Feeling bad about yourself and having negative thoughts may be the way you do things now, but you can change that. It will take an effort on your part to stop negative thinking and begin positive thinking. When you do, though, you'll be on your way to putting yourself in charge of your habits.

Often, other people try to put themselves in charge of your eating. Adults sometimes think they can simply tell you to stop overeating. It's not that easy; if it were, there wouldn't be so many overweight boys and girls.

Many overweight children who work with counselors and doctors have parents who try to control their eating habits. These children often raid the cupboards quietly in order to take charge of their own choices. Like some of the children discussed in Chapter 1, they reach for food when they need to swallow their anger, fear, sadness, loneliness, or boredom.

But children who take charge by secret eating have another choice. They can develop new behaviors in place of the old, comfortable eating habits they have. To change, they must *think* about their actions, *decide* if that action is right, and *choose* a new action if that action isn't right.

Here's an example. Let's say that you always grab a cookie or two from the cookie jar every time you're in the kitchen. Grabbing cookies is a habit; you don't really think about it, you just do it.

To change this habit, you must make yourself think about what you're doing each and every time you do it. Before you grab a cookie or a snack, you have to take time to ask, "Am I really hungry right now?" Check out how your stomach feels before you go ahead and eat your treat.

There are lots of things you might do while you're trying to decide whether to eat. Maybe you could make up some rules for yourself: "I will walk in and out of the kitchen three times before I let myself take a treat," or, "When I want a snack,

EATING CLOCK

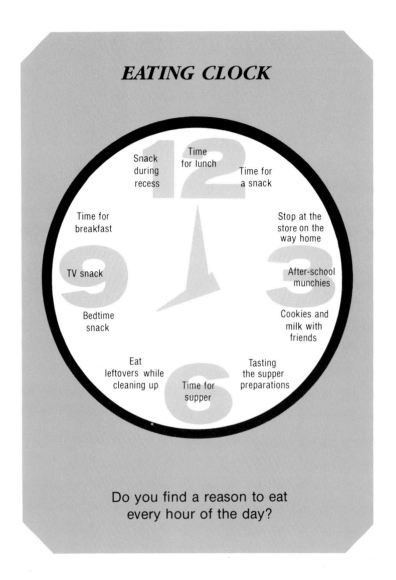

Snack during recess

Time for lunch

Time for a snack

Time for breakfast

Stop at the store on the way home

TV snack

After-school munchies

Bedtime snack

Cookies and milk with friends

Eat leftovers while cleaning up

Tasting the supper preparations

Time for supper

**Do you find a reason to eat
every hour of the day?**

I will set a timer for ten minutes. I can't eat the treat until the timer goes off." Whatever rule you make, be sure you give yourself a little time to think about eating.

By building in time to make a decision, you put yourself in charge of your eating. When you think, choose, and decide about food, you are being responsible for what you're doing.

The chances are good that you won't always remember to ask yourself your questions. That's okay. It's important not to get angry with yourself when you overeat. Changing any habit takes time and lots of hard work. Every day that you do it, you get more and more practice at good habits. When you're working on changes, you can only work on them one day at a time!

Be sure to forgive yourself when you overeat.

You're going to have to help everyone learn about the new you.

CHAPTER 3

Talking About the New You

By this point, you have looked at some of the reasons that you overeat, you've decided you can change, and you're not going to be too critical of yourself while you're working on taking charge. Let's talk now about how to discuss your new resolutions about eating with your family and friends.

Often, parents show their children they love them by buying or baking treats. Dad may say "I love you" with a box of doughnuts. Mother might say "I love you" with a trip to the park and a steady supply of hot dogs, french fries, and milk shakes.

You want to show you appreciate their attention, and the food does taste good. So, you keep eating and eating, even though you were full an hour ago. They watch you eat and think they have shown you how much they love you. Giving and sharing food is one of life's pleasures.

Tell them you love them, and you know they love you, but from now on, the ways of showing it can't include food. Practice saying things like "I love you, Dad, but I don't want any doughnuts" or "I love you,

Mom, but I'd rather throw the Frisbee than eat now."

Changing habits is difficult for everyone. It will be hard for your family to break the habit of offering food. You will have to say over and over, "Thank you, I'm full" and "No, thank you." Experts say you must repeat a new rule at least three times before people really hear it. Be prepared to say patiently, "No, thank you," many, many times. Your way of accepting love has changed, and you're going to have to help everyone learn about the "new you."

Tell Dad you'd rather go bicycling with him, or swim laps at the YMCA, or work a puzzle than sit around eating. Tell Mom you'd like to go to a movie or hike somewhere with her.

You can't expect your parents to read your mind. Explain about losing weight. Ask them to do the things you would like to do. Sometimes when you're watching television or talking to a friend, you might get an idea about some activity you'd like to do. Remember it and later write it down. Keep your list handy; then, when Mom or Dad asks what you would like to do (instead of sitting around eating treats), you will have an idea list already prepared.

Using your list, you can say, "Do you remember when Uncle Brady told us how he planted pumpkin seeds in his back yard? I'd like to make a place and plant pumpkins, too." Or tell them, "Do you re-member that I decided to walk around the block three times every day? Would you walk with me?" "Do you remember that I wanted to learn more about butterflies? Can we go to the bookstore or library and find a good book on the subject?" The world is full of wonderful things to do.

Maybe you just want them to tell you they love you. Tell them. Say something like this: "I love you, Dad. How much do you love me?" or "Do you love me, Mom? I love you a whole lot."

Another thing that makes it hard to stick to a controlled eating program is a "clean your plate" attitude. Your parents fill your plate, then tell you to clean it up. They measure how much your stom-ach can hold by their own stomachs. They may have grown up in a time when food was less plentiful than it is today. Remembering that time, they are unwilling to throw out uneaten food, and they want all the food on the serving plate to be eaten. In other cases, parents feel it is a measure of suc-cess to provide large amounts of good things to eat.

If Mom or Dad tells you to clean up your plate, say, "I'm full. I'm learning to control my eating." Be polite but firm. (On the other hand, you must be honest about why you are full. If you ate a triple ice

Asking Your Parents to Help

1. Give me choices. Have a variety of fruits and vegetables available to eat.

2. Trust me not to sneak food. Please allow me to have privacy in my room by not checking for hidden snacks.

3. Think of activities we can do together that don't include food.

4. Listen when I say I'm full, and avoid encouraging me to eat more.

5. Don't buy junk food.

6. Say anything good about my appearance. I need all the support I can get.

7. Love and accept me the way I am, while I am trying to change.

8. Unless you know how to help me with a sensible eating program, please make an appointment for me with a doctor or nutritionist.

9. If we can't talk together about the issue of my overeating, help me find someone I can talk to.

10. Hug me. Tell me you know how tough it is to change old habits, and that you're proud of my efforts.

cream cone on the way home from ball practice, and you expect your mom or dad to throw out your salad because you can't eat it, he or she has a right to feel upset! The truth is, most kids do not get fat because they eat all the food on their plates. They do so because they eat too many treats before and after mealtime.) Only you know when you have had enough to eat. You may have to say ten times, "No, thank you. I'm full." Ask Mom or Dad ahead of time not to put so much food on your plate. Ask them not to prepare so much food for you, because you are trying to learn to eat less.

Tell them when they are confusing you. They might seem to be saying, "Don't get fat, but keep overeating." Say to them that one dip of ice cream is as much of a treat as three. Two potato chips are enough. And half a biscuit is plenty.

When you change your attitude about eating, you'll also have to explain the "new you" to your friends. You'll have to practice telling them what this "new you" needs. Often, people who have a habit of overeating also have a habit of spending too much time trying to please others. They put their own wishes last. They leave their needs out.

For someone not used to it, speaking up to parents, older people, bigger kids, or kids who seem smarter takes courage. Asking someone to think about what you want may seem hard. Perhaps you think that these people will say, "Do things my way or forget about doing anything with me at all." So you go along with activities you think are boring or stupid. You may feel the only thing you can control in your afternoon is the number of chips you eat.

Take charge in a new way. Speak up in a pleasant voice and say what you would like to do. You may get to do what you want some of the time, and some of the time you may not. By giving everyone a chance to decide on activities, you and your friends will all learn new things. Make a bargain, if you can. Say, "This time we will play your game, next time we will play mine." Then, when next time comes, speak up: "Remember, today it's my turn to decide what we will do." For instance, if your friend wants to go swimming one morning, say, "Okay, if we can go roller skating tomorrow afternoon, I will go swimming with you this morning."

Learn to talk to your friends about feeling cornered. Tell them when you feel that everyone else is making decisions for you. Don't accuse, just discuss the problem. Perhaps your friend often feels that way, too. You'll find it's better for your overeating control plan if you talk about the times you feel trapped rather than eating because you're angry.

Another thing you will have to change is the habit of buying treats to make and keep friends.

Suppose someone wants to show you a good time, so he or she insists you both go to the soda shop for a sundae. This person thinks you will only be a friend as long as he or she buys you treats. You feel that this person will be your friend only as long as you eat the treats.

This is another difficult situation. Before now, each of you knows how the other will act when you get together. Now you are going to change the things you do to share friendship. You are no longer going to spend all of your money on treats for others. Also, you will not allow friends to spend their money on treats for you. You are going to ask them to think of other things to do together.

Real friends can't be bought with ice cream. If your friend does not want to help you change, you may have to find another friend whose interests are things other than food. There's a whole big world of things to do, and eating is only one of them.

Please yourself with a new control over your eating habits, and be sure that your family and friends understand what you are doing.

Sometimes it's harder to take charge when a family has serious problems.

CHAPTER 4

Special Pressure

Often, children who overeat find that they have special problems at home. Sometimes their families say things, or do things, or expect things that make them feel pressured. Sometimes it's harder to take charge when a family has serious problems.

There are thoughtless people in the world who may call you names. Often, this is because they are having problems in their own lives, and don't know how to deal with them. It's as if you came home and kicked your dog every time you got a poor grade in math. Some of these "kick" names are stupid, fatso, dummy, blimp, clumsy, simple, and other names you've heard.

The word *thoughtless* means "not thinking." Thoughtless people do not think about the words they use hurting others. You can tell them when they're thoughtless. Say, "Stop calling me names. That hurts my feelings." But suppose it is your parents or a brother or sister who is saying the hurtful things. It might be harder to speak up.

Why does this happen? Sometimes, parents

don't know how to deal with their feelings in a useful way. They may even think they are not good parents. Then, they act the way you might when you're unhappy: they speak out and hurt people who are not to blame for their bad feelings. Brothers and sisters can have bad feelings about themselves, too.

In this case, whether they mean it or not, family members may give you the idea they don't want you to be more successful than they are. They may say, or make you feel they have said, "You can't be better than me. You'll never amount to anything. You're no good."

If you hear someone in your family telling you this, say to yourself, "I am good. I will amount to something. I am smart. I am lovable." Say it and believe it.

Parents, brothers, or sisters don't mean to tell you you shouldn't be smart in math just because they aren't. You may be able to understand science, computers, or poetry that baffles them. That's okay. There are things they know that you haven't had a chance to learn yet. Maybe you can teach each other new things, and then you will all be smarter.

Are you afraid that your family and friends will laugh when you speak up about being overweight and feeling pressure? How will you know unless you try? Here are some ways to start a discussion.

- *To begin, don't use angry talk. Keep your voice tone quiet.*

- *Choose a time when you can have your parent's, brother's, or sister's full attention. Don't begin talking about your feelings while Mom is watching the Superbowl or Dad and your sister are trying to outguess the players on a favorite game show.*

- *Talk about your own feelings only. Don't accuse others. Say, "I feel hurt," not, "You hurt me." Say, "I feel bad when you say those words to me," not, "You are mean when you say those things." Tell them, "I don't like it when you force me to eat," not, "You can't make me eat that."*

- *Above all, do not start a quarrel. You are trying to stop the name calling, not restart it.*

If your parents are unable to let you talk about your feelings (and this may happen—they may think you are being sassy or backtalking), then you may try writing a letter to your mother or father to explain your feelings. That way, he or she can think about the situation without making an instant misjudgment of what you're trying to say. You could also try sharing this book with them.

Talking about yourself is hard. On the other hand, being hurt by name calling is hard, too. We suggest that you try to talk to name callers. You never know—talking like this often works.

There are quite a few family situations where you may seem to have no choices. One of the things you'll have to practice, in addition to taking charge, is seeing the choices in your life. Here are some examples.

If both your parents work, your family may eat out a lot. As a result, there may not be much food in your house except snack foods. Your choices: You can take some responsibility for shopping and for preparing foods you can eat and not gain extra weight with. You may have to ask for fruits, vegetables, and other low-calorie treats when groceries are bought. (In the appendix you will find some useful information on learning to shop.)

Some parents have so much to do at work that they don't feel much like beginning another job, as cook, when they get home. Your choice: You could help out on cooking chores. Instead of always eating out or bringing home already-prepared food, your family might like it if you offered to prepare a wonderful salad and serve it for supper.

There are choices even if you do eat out a lot. You can try sticking to salads or to fish or chicken dishes. You can eat things that are prepared in a simple way—broiling, grilling, boiling, baking, and poaching. You can avoid foods that are deep-fried, fried, or covered with cheese or a gooey sauce. If you get a huge plate of food in a restaurant, eat some of the food, but stop when you're full.

Another situation: If Mom or Dad thinks being fat means being healthy, you probably will have a hard time convincing her or him otherwise. They may tell you that you'll grow out of your fat—and they may be right, unless you continue to overeat into adulthood. Explain to your family that you want to be sure that you aren't fat all of your life. By getting control of your eating habits now, you can grow into a normal-size adult and look and feel better right now.

If your parents are out of control of their own lives, you might find it difficult to discuss anything with them. Some parents use too much alcohol, drugs, or food themselves. They may have addictions, and may need professional help. If they have these problems, it is unlikely they want to hear you talk about them.

Your parents aren't the only people who can help you change. You can talk to another relative, a minister, a priest, a sister, a social worker, a teacher, a school counselor, or another adult you trust. They will help you themselves, or help you find people who can offer you advice and support concerning the situation in your home.

You cannot solve your parents' problems by overeating. If your parents have addictions, you will have to be responsible for yourself and solve your overeating problems without their help. Some parents like their addictions and do not want to change. You cannot change them. You can only change yourself. Don't bother whining, criticizing, or complaining about them. Change almost always has to come through a choice. Here, it's your choice, not your parents'.

There are other family situations that don't deal directly with food and eating habits, but which often trigger overeating. For instance, sometimes parents put other pressure on their children. They may be constantly telling their children what to do. These parents give their children many jobs around the house. Chores, chores, chores. Is that the way it is at your house?

Your choice: You can tell your parents you

want to help at home, but you need time for your-self to relax, to be alone, and to be with friends, too. Ask your parents if it would be possible to have at least thirty minutes after school to do anything you want. Then, you will get to the chores. Maybe you can make a list of things you are supposed to do, and put beside each item the amount of time you need to complete the chore. If you show this to your parents, you probably can work out a time for a break. Then use this break time for something you want to do. (But stay out of the kitchen until it's time to help with supper!)

Maybe your parents want to dress you up in clothes in a certain style, the sort they didn't have but wanted when they were your age, and you hate that type of clothes. Maybe they wanted to play the piano when they were young, and you hate the piano. But, you have to learn to play it anyway. Maybe you are expected to be a star in sports, and you don't like that sort of rough activity. You may not know how to tell them you don't want to do those things, so you eat and eat; you're good at eating.

If you feel trapped, you are going to have to talk to your parents about the things they want for you, and the things you want for yourself. But be truthful. Do not dislike the activities they

Upside-Down Thinking

Fat people are happy and jolly.

I'm fat because my parents are fat.

I eat like a bird.

The way to lose weight is to starve yourself.

Drinking water makes you weigh more.

Exercise must make me really tired to be any good.

I'm not fat, I'm pleasingly plump.

I'm big boned.

My overweight is caused by a gland problem.

I'll grow out of this baby fat.

Right Side Up Answers

Fat people are called names and left out of games. They are not happy and jolly about that. They are not happy about the look of their round bodies, either.

About 50 percent of children who are fat have fat parents. But that means 50 percent do not.

Birds eat *half their weight* in seeds or bugs every day. Do you?

When you stop eating as a method of dieting, your body will hang on to the energy (calories) that it does have. You will have to go without food longer to lose the same amount of weight you would lose if you ate a sensible diet.

Water does not contain calories and passes through the body quickly.

The best exercise is fast walking. It's safer, easier, and better than aerobics or jogging.

If you are overweight, you are not pleasingly fat (another word for plump). No one is pleased—least of all *you*.

Saying you're big boned is another excuse (like plump).

Less than two percent of people who are fat have gland or other medical problems. Mostly their problem is one of overeating and under-exercising. However, overweight caused by a medical problem is treatable. Your doctor will know.

People who are fat as children have more fat cells as adults; therefore, they have a harder time controlling over-weight. It is important to keep your weight close to normal during childhood, to prevent overweight as an adult.

choose just because they chose them, or refuse to wear the clothes they like just because you don't want anything they might like. Try their idea first.

Then, if it doesn't work out, say, "I tried that sport and I couldn't make the team. I'm not good enough at it and don't enjoy playing it." Or, "I know you spent a lot of money on piano (clarinet, trumpet, violin) lessons, but I don't like to play music. I do not mean to disappoint you, but I have tried, and not succeeded in playing well enough for anyone to enjoy it."

Remember the guidelines for having a good discussion with your parents—pick a good time; don't argue; talk about *your* feelings without accusing anyone.

There's another reason that boys and girls feel pressure that results in overeating. Sometimes, things go wrong in a family. Parents may not get along with one another. Maybe they disagree and argue. You might feel it's your fault they quarrel all the time.

You need to know that all people in relationships disagree occasionally. Ask your parents if you are the reason they are quarreling; chances are, they will be surprised that the thought even occurred to you. Tell them about your fears. You may be afraid they are going to get a divorce. Even if that happens, that's not your fault. You can't keep their marriage together by overeating. If they do split up, they're leaving each other. It is NOT your fault.

Perhaps your parents move often, and you dislike leaving old friends and making new ones. All the doughnuts in the world will not help. If your parents need to move, you will have to adjust to a new town and school.

Another situation that is harder to talk about, and may not be understood at first, is jealousy in a parent. At the same time a girl begins to change into a lovely young woman, her mother may begin to feel older and less attractive. Mothers who feel this way may behave in a way that embarrasses or hurts their daughters. Fathers can have problems with jealousy, too. A father may act jealous when a son gets special attention from his mother. The father feels left out.

Parents need to deal with this problem themselves; feelings of jealousy are normal in all of us. They may not know they are trapping you in the middle. Say, "I feel in the middle. Mom/Dad is playing cards with me, and you seem not to like that." You could say, "I love you, Mom/Dad, even though I'm going to the park with Dad/Mom."

If you've tried to talk to your parents, and you just haven't been able to get anywhere, try writing them a note or letter. Parents can feel rejected, just as kids do. They might be uncomfortable or threatened when faced with problems. It may not have anything to do with reality, but they feel that way just the same.

If family situations get to be more than you can deal with, you might talk to another adult with whom you feel comfortable. Eating until your stomach hurts will not solve the issues, but a talk with someone who can offer you encouragement might. The people around you will be able to give you lots of help when they know you need it. Ask. Explain. They will understand.

There's another person in your family who might be putting a lot of pressure on you—you yourself. Some people eat more than they need when they feel disappointed in themselves. They feel a sweet treat will cheer them up. Or the opposite may be true: they punish themselves for not doing what they and their families expect by eating and overeating.

To sum it up: When you feel flattened by pressure, there are many things you can do. You can try talking, writing notes and letters, sharing this book, or visiting a counselor or other adult. If you still feel that family issues are unsolved, you can sit down and write a note to yourself. Write about your bad feelings and your fears. Sometimes, writing things on paper makes them look less scary.

You are a winner for doing something about the problem. Although you may not be able to solve family problems today or even tomorrow, you can be in charge of the way you respond to those problems.

Tell yourself that you're not going to eat when you feel cornered. Then, look for other ways to ease your frustrations—take a long walk, ride your bike, beat up a pillow, or even write a letter to someone you're angry with, then rip it into tiny shreds. When you're calmer, remind yourself of your successes and your good points. Give yourself, and your family, time. If you looked at a list of today's troubles six months from now, you might be surprised to see how time has solved some of them.

There are special situations where your eating habits will be put to the test.

CHAPTER 5

The Social Squeeze

There are special situations when your new eating habits will be put to the test. Some of the situations can be fun—going to a carnival, a birthday party, or a family holiday dinner, for instance. Some can possibly make you feel down—shopping for clothes and not finding what you want in your size; being picked on by a thoughtless person; or just comparing yourself to the perfect faces and bodies you see on TV.

We can't say it often enough: you can be in charge of how you act. You have choices. From time to time you may fail to make a choice and rely on old habits. That's okay, because everyone goes backwards sometimes. But when you do remember to choose, you're building a good habit. That habit can help you keep weight off for the rest of your life.

Here are some suggestions for situations that might seem like a "social squeeze."

• Parties: At parties, food that is bite-size, salty, sugary, or creamy is often handy. The food is meant to be part of the fun. Before you took charge of your eating, this food would have seemed wonderful to you. Now, your self-control will be tested. Can you get through the party without overeating?

It might be difficult to keep away from the snacks and dips if you haven't eaten before going to the party. Try having an apple or another low-calorie goodie before you go. When you get to the party, have a tall glass of water to help fill you up. The best thing of all is to find something else to do besides eating. Talk to the other people at the party. Find out about them and their experiences. Show interest in them instead of the party goodies.

If someone says, "Aren't you eating?" tell them that you're already full. A tip: it's best if you don't announce to everyone that you are trying to control your weight. People on these occasions say, "Oh, have just a little. One won't hurt."

One may not hurt, but if it is a sweet, sugary treat, it may cause you to eat another and another. Sugar, especially, is addicting for some people. The more these people eat, the more they want to eat. It's our experience that once you start, it's hard to get off this eating circle.

• Holiday dinners: People like to celebrate holidays and important events with rich, tasty food, and lots of it. Part of our social traditions in this country revolve around foods—wedding cakes, Christmas dinners, Thanksgiving turkeys with stuffing, candy for Valentine's Day, and so on. You can probably think of a long list.

The pressure to eat a whole lot on these occasions will be hard to resist. Do your best. If you do get carried away with all the special food, don't feel guilty. The next day, go back to your good eating habits and keep trying.

Let's say that sweets are your weakness. Rather than feel left out because of your choice not to eat a lot, perhaps you should have a small piece of a single dessert. Then tell everyone else and yourself, "I'm full. I can't eat any more. No, thank you." Don't feel guilty about refusing to overeat, and don't give in. If you do give in, people will continue to push food at you. They won't believe you when you say you're full the next time, either.

Try to keep away from the food. Think of things you can do when family and friends gather for a celebration. Talk to some of the older people and find out what things were like for them when they were children. Offer to help prepare the vegetables. Play games with your cousins and friends. And no matter what you are eating, stop when you are full.

• Shopping for clothes: It's easy to feel down when you have to buy a larger size than other kids your age, or when you really want a style of clothes that only comes in small sizes. Being depressed often leads to overeating.

You'll have to make a special effort to remember your promise—not to say mean things to or about yourself. Say, "This is the size I wear now, but I will be getting thinner. Then I will wear the same size as my friends wear."

If someone makes fun of your clothing size, tell that person he or she is hurting your feelings. Perhaps you can agree with them and say, "I know I'm overweight." Many times, agreeing with a critical person will stop the criticism. Remember, people who are critical, who measure the good qualities in people by the size of their clothes, miss many good times and good friendships.

Don't let these people keep you down. Wear clothing that feels good on you today; then, go ahead and enjoy the activities you like. Don't put off having fun because of your body size or because of hurtful things that people say. The more fun you have, the better you will feel. That makes it easier to avoid situations in which you overeat. The size of your swimming suit has nothing to do with the hours of fun you can have swimming. The sun shines on everyone.

• Comparisons: Whether anyone says it or not, there's a lot of pressure on everyone to look like the people appearing on TV and in advertising. Many times these people are held up as ideals of male or female beauty. You may feel sad that you don't look like a model or a movie superstar.

There's something you should know about those "ideal" people: a lot of time, money, and makeup goes into making them look good. They're dressed in custom-made clothes and posed to make those clothes look good. Special cameras and lighting are used to make those people seem perfect. It's a full-time job to be ideal-looking!

The people who love you want you to look your best—but not like some plastic stranger. You are a special blend of your heredity, of who your parents and their parents are. You cannot change this. You are a good, lovable person. When your weight is normal, you will feel even better about yourself.

Styles change. One year long hair is in, another year curly hair is popular. One year it's jeans, another year it's the preppy look. But a healthy body is always in style.

Quiz

1. Do you hate the way you look?
   a. Yes, always
   b. Sometimes
   c. No

2. Do you eat until you are uncomfortable?
   a. Every day
   b. Sometimes
   c. Hardly ever

3. Do you sneak food from the cupboard or refrigerator?
   a. Often
   b. Sometimes
   c. Almost never

4. Do you hide food in your room?
   a. Yes
   b. Sometimes
   c. No

5. Do you eat too much?
   a. Yes, every day
   b. Sometimes
   c. Not usually

6. Do you eat when you're not hungry?
   a. Usually
   b. Once in a while
   c. Almost never

7. Do you save your lunch money to buy treats for friends?
   a. Often
   b. Once in a while
   c. No

8. Do you dream that someday you will magically lose weight?
   a. Yes
   b. Sometimes
   c. No

Every "a" answer points out a behavior that works against overeating control. Try to use the suggestions we have presented in Part I to help you change these behaviors. Try to put yourself in charge of your eating. If, after trying for several weeks, you still are answering "a" to half these questions, you may have to ask for help from a counselor, a minister, the school nurse, a health teacher, a doctor, a relative, or any other adult you can trust who will listen and offer suggestions.

Say, "I'm wonderful." Say it loud enough to hear with your own ears. Then believe it. People tend to believe things they hear. They also tend to behave in the way they think they are expected to behave. As a wonderful person, you can act proud of yourself!

Now that you have heard that you are wonderful and know you are expected to behave like a wonderful person, you will be able to stand up to the social pressure that once made you feel bad.

In this section, Part I, we have talked about reasons for overeating, both because of what you tell yourself and because of how other people act. In the next section, we will talk about the basics of diet, nutrition, exercise, and behavior changes you can make to help you on your way to a healthy, normal-weight body.

Part II

Working Toward the Solution

You can become an expert on the
foods you eat.

CHAPTER 6

Food, Fuel for Life

Although stomachs don't have fuel gauges to tell you when they're almost empty, they do send signals to your head. Learn to recognize and pay attention to these signals. The best way to know if you are truly hungry is to think about your body's needs. Do you feel weak? Is your stomach growling? Does it ache? Are you feeling empty? These are the ways your body tells you to send food, because its supply of nutrients is getting low.

Suppose you recognize these hunger signals, but you send foods that do not supply your body with the right things for carrying on. It can't say, "No, not potato chips. I need green vegetables and ripe fruit. No, not cola. I need milk. I need juice." Your stomach will continue to send hunger signals. If you keep eating foods that do not supply its wants, or do so only in small amounts, you will take in a great amount of calories before you get enough nutrients to make your stomach shut off the signal system.

Nutritious foods do more than just fill your stomach and satisfy your urge to munch. They provide calories, minerals and vitamins, proteins, fats, and carbohydrates. Your body values these more than flavor. These keep your body running smoothly, and help you maintain normal weight.

Bodies get energy from the calories in foods you eat. Calories are measurements of the energy that food can provide. The calories in a peanut butter sandwich will give you enough working energy to run around the block several times. If, however, you eat the sandwich and don't run around the block, your body will save the energy-producing calories for a time when you will be running. If you continue to eat without exercising, these calories will be stored as fat in fat cells scattered around your body. The fat cells will grow and grow, ballooning out with all that "energy" you're storing.

Not only will each cell grow larger, but the number of cells will increase. Once these fat cells are in place, they never go away. It's important not to have too many of them. Because their normal state is to be full of fat, they will tend to store fat for the rest of your life. Fat cells added to your body in childhood make it very difficult to be a normal-weight adult.

Nearly all foods have some calories, but many foods have large amounts of calories. Usually these foods are pleasing to eat, but low in nutrition.

Junk Foods

These have very little nutritional value.
Some are high in sugar.
Some are high in fat.
All are high in calories.
EAT ONLY IN SMALL AMOUNTS,
OR NOT AT ALL!

Many people call these "junk foods," because of the low quality of their nutrients.

Food also contains vitamins and minerals, which are needed for good health. Vitamins are called A, B, C, D, and E. Some of the B vitamins have numbers behind them to set them apart from other B vitamins: B_1, B_6, B_{12}, etc. The best sources of these are fruits and vegetables. At the end of this book is an appendix showing which vegetables provide these vitamins.

Minerals have some of the same names as soil

minerals: calcium, iron, sodium, zinc, potassium, phosphorus, and so on. Just as plants grow better in soils that have the right minerals, so bodies grow better with the right food minerals. The best sources of food minerals are milk, meat, and whole grains, as well as vegetables.

Another important part of food is called protein. Protein helps bodies form muscles, glands, hair, fingernails, skin, blood, and almost every part of you. The protein your cells use up needs to be replaced every day with other high-quality proteins gotten from the foods you eat. Excellent sources of protein are beef, eggs, fish, peanuts, dried beans, chicken, cottage cheese, and lamb.

Foods also contain carbohydrates. Carbohydrates are made up of sugars and starches. The best sugars for your body come packaged in wrappers with eye-catching colors: purple (grapes and and figs); yellow (bananas and peaches); orange (oranges and apricots); red (apples, plums, cherries, and strawberries); green (watermelon). Just open these packages and eat what's inside. In some cases, the package is good to eat, too.

Starches are the other kind of carbohydrates. The best starches come in whole grains and cereals, such as wheat, rice, oats, and corn. There's also

a nongrain food that has excellent starches—
potatoes. These foods with starches are usually
baked or cooked into other forms, such as spaghetti, macaroni, bread, breakfast cereal, grits,
mush, cooked rice, and granola.

Carbohydrates provide the working power for
your body, including the power to think. They
also provide fiber, to keep the parts of you that
digest your food humming along like a perfectly
oiled machine.

Fats, another part of many foods, are necessary to keep your body system well tuned. Fats make
your skin healthy and help your digestive system
work smoothly. They are found mostly in the milk-
meat categories of foods. Examples are cream,
whole milk, butter, bacon, hamburger, and pork.
Vegetable fats are found in nuts and seeds. Examples are sunflower seeds, peanuts, and palm and
coconut oils, which are used in salad dressings and margarine. Shortening made from vegetable products is used in baking and frying.

However, fats are also high in calories and
must be eaten in small amounts if you are going to
keep your body weight normal. Some doctors be-
believe eating fat helps clog your arteries, leading to
blood circulation problems later, in adulthood.

Bread-Cereal Group

Sources: Rolls ★ Nonsweetened Cereal ★
Whole-wheat Bread ★ Spaghetti ★
Pancakes ★ Tortillas ★ Corn Bread ★
Rice ★ Macaroni ★

Servings: You need four or more servings from
this group every day.
Examples of a single serving:
One slice of bread
One medium pancake
Five crackers
One tortilla
One bowl of cereal
One bowl of cooked rice, noodles, or
spaghetti

Vegetable-Fruit Group

Sources: Cantaloupe ★ Broccoli ★ Spinach ★
Lettuce ★ Celery ★ Cucumbers ★
Apples ★ Strawberries ★ Corn ★
Peas ★ Pears ★ Potatoes ★

Servings: You need four or more servings from
this group every day.
Examples of a single serving:
One piece of fresh fruit
Half a grapefruit
One-quarter cantaloupe
One helping of salad
One medium potato

Fabulous Food Groups

Meat Group

Sources: Chicken ★ Beef ★ Lamb ★ Pork ★
Eggs ★ Fish ★ Peanuts ★ Beans ★
Split Peas ★

Servings: You need two or more servings from
this group every day.

Examples of a single serving:
One hamburger patty
One pork chop
One lamb chop
One bowl of beans
One piece of fish
Two eggs
One large slice of chicken, ham,
    roast beef, or meatloaf

Milk Group

Sources: Milk ★ Cheese ★ Yogurt ★ Custard ★
Pudding ★ Buttermilk ★

Servings: You need three or more servings
every day from this group.

Examples of a single serving:
One glass of milk
One small carton of yogurt
Two slices of cheese

*Note: This chart is a guide, not a complete list of
every food in each group. The best diet has a wide
variety of foods in it that are eaten in normal-size
portions.*

Clogged arteries can also help create heart problems and strokes.

Try to restrict the fats you eat to those occurring naturally in foods like nuts, meats, and cheeses. Avoid those that you pile on other foods, such as butter on vegetables, popcorn, and bread; bacon fat on eggs and potatoes; cream on fruits; chocolate on nuts; and creamy salad dressings on fresh lettuce. Fat on food makes it seem tastier, but beware—it's the same fat that will fill your fat cells.

Now, how will you know what kind of nutrition is in a food? There are calorie charts handy in libraries and in the backs of most cookbooks. There are lists on the labels of canned and packaged foods. There are charts of minerals and vitamins, and lists of what to eat in many magazines. People everywhere want to know how to improve their diets and get more nutrition for their food intake. In Chapter 10 we've written about some books that will give you more information on these subjects.

Talk to your doctor. Talk to your health teacher. Talk to the librarian. You can become an expert on the foods you eat.

Foods wrapped in nature's packages aren't labeled, but the government requires manufacturers to prepare such labels. In this chapter we show some manufacturers' labels. Notice how many times these words for sugar are listed: sugar, brown sugar, sucrose, corn syrup, honey. Notice the fats: hydrogenated vegetable oil, cocoa butter. Notice the other words you probably can't pronounce, and don't know what they mean. These are often terms for preservatives, spoilage retardants, artificial flavorings and colorings, and stabilizers. These ingredients make the food so distasteful to insects and bacteria that it will stay in the same condition on a shelf for six months or more. This long shelf life is an advantage for manufacturers, because fewer things spoil, but the chemicals put into these foods do nothing for your body. Can you imagine what a peach would look like after six months on a warm shelf?

We've found the best idea is to read labels (it's boring at first) and try to avoid foods containing ingredients that you can't pronounce, never heard of, and don't know about. When you get the hang of it, you'll find knowing about nutrition is fun. After all, you deserve the very best in food. You want only the best fuel for your number one machine—your very own body.

Label Reading Practice

1.

INGREDIENTS: ROLLED OATS, PEANUT BUTTER, PEANUTS, SUCROSE, HYDROGENATED VEGETABLE OIL (COTTONSEED AND/OR RAPESEED AND/OR PALM OIL), SALT, CRISP RICE (RICE, SUGAR, SALT, MALT), INVERT SUGAR, BROWN SUGAR, ROLLED WHOLE WHEAT, CORN SYRUP, HONEY, CORN SYRUP SOLIDS, GLYCERIN, NONFAT DRY MILK, DRIED UNSWEETENED COCONUT, ALMONDS, SALT, NATURAL AND ARTIFICIAL FLAVORS, BHA (A PRESERVATIVE), CITRIC ACID (A STABILIZING AGENT).

NUTRITION INFORMATION	
SERVING SIZE	1 oz.
SERVS./CONTAINER	8
CALORIES	130
PROTEIN	3 g
CARBOHYDRATE	18 g
FAT	5 g
SODIUM	175 mg/serving
POTASSIUM	80 mg/serving

2.

PURE VEGETABLE OIL
NO CHOLESTEROL

NUTRITIONAL INFORMATION (PER SERVING): SERVING SIZE: 1 TABLESPOON: 14g...SERVINGS PER CONTAINER: 48... CALORIES: 120... PROTEIN: 0 g...CARBOHYDRATE: 0 g... FAT: 14 g... CHOLESTEROL: 0 mg (0 mg PER 100 g)...SODIUM: 0 mg (0 mg/100 g)

PARTIALLY HYDROGENATED SOYBEAN OIL, POLYGLYCERIDES

3.

INGREDIENTS: SUGAR, GELATIN, SODIUM CITRATE (CONTROLS ACIDITY), FUMARIC ACID, NATURAL AND ARTIFICIAL FLAVOR, SALT, ASCORBIC ACID (VITAMIN C), ARTIFICIAL COLOR (CONTAINS FD&C YELLOW NO. 5).

4.

WHOLE KERNEL
SWEET CORN

NET WEIGHT: 482 GRAMS*
INGREDIENTS: WHOLE KERNEL CORN, WATER, SUGAR, SALT.
SERVING DIRECTIONS: HEAT; SEASON TO TASTE; SERVE.

NUTRITION INFORMATION PER SERVING	
SERVING SIZE .... ½ CUP	
SERVINGS PER CONTAINER ..... APPROX. 4	
CALORIES 80	FAT 1g
PROTEIN 2g	SODIUM ... 300mg
CARBOHYDRATE ... 18g	

*WEIGHT OF CORN BEFORE ADDITION OF LIQUID NECESSARY FOR PROCESSING.

When reading a label, remember the ingredients are listed in order of amount. For example, the first label lists rolled oats first. There are more rolled oats in this food than the second listed item, peanut butter.

Things to find out from these labels:

1. Which label came from a can containing more corn than water or salt?
2. Per serving, which foods have the most calories?

chocolate bar

NUTRITION INFORMATION PER SERVING

SERV SIZE .... ½ BAR   SERV/BAR ... 2
CALORIES 170
PROTEIN .... 4 grams
CARBOHYDRATES .... 15 grams
  SUGARS .... 13 grams
  OTHER CARBOHYDRATES ....2 grams
FAT .... 10 grams

INGREDIENTS: MILK CHOCOLATE (MILK CHOCOLATE CONTAINS SUGAR; COCOA BUTTER; MILK; CHOCOLATE; SOYA LECITHIN, AN EMULSIFIER; AND VANILLIN, AN ARTIFICIAL FLAVORING) AND PEANUTS.

NUTRITION INFORMATION PER SERVING

SERVING SIZE .... 4 OZ. - CONDENSED
        (8 OZ. AS PREPARED - 226 g)
SERVINGS PER CONTAINER 2¾

	AS PACKAGED	WITH MILK
CALORIES	90	 160
PROTEIN (GRAMS)................	1	 5
TOTAL CARBOHYDRATES (GRAMS)	17	 22
SIMPLE SUGARS (GRAMS)	10	 15
COMPLEX CARBOHYDRATES (GRAMS)	7	 7
FAT (GRAMS).....................	2	 6
SODIUM	760mg/serving	810mg/serving

INGREDIENTS: TOMATOES, CORN SYRUP, WHEAT FLOUR, SALT, PARTIALLY HYDROGENATED VEGETABLE OILS (SOYBEAN OR COTTONSEED OIL), NATURAL FLAVORING, ASCORBIC ACID (VITAMIN C) AND CITRIC ACID.

TO CLOSE PUSH HERE

7.

FORTIFIED WITH 6 ESSENTIAL VITAMINS PLUS IRON

NUTRITION INFORMATION (Per Serving)

SERVING SIZE: 1 Packet (1¼ oz.)

	1 Pkt. Cereal (1¼ oz)	With 2 Oz Whole Milk
Calories	130	170
Protein (g)	2	4
Carbohydrate (g)	30	33
Fat (g)	0	2
Sodium (mg)	220	250

INGREDIENTS:
Farina, Brown Sugar, Sugar, Dehydrated Apples, Guar Gum, Wheat Germ, Salt, Calcium Carbonate, Cinnamon, Natural Flavor, Malic Acid, Caramel Color (Vegetable Color), Reduced Iron, Partially Hydrogenated Soybean Oil, Niacin, BHA (Preservative), Vitamin A Acetate, Pyridoxine Hydrochloride (Vitamin B_6), Mono and Diglycerides, Thiamine Mononitrate (Vitamin B_1), Riboflavin (Vitamin B_2), Folic Acid (a B-Vitamin).

---

3. According to which label was Yellow Number 5 used as an artificial color?
4. Which labels say that sugar, in any form, is an ingredient?
5. Which has the most sodium (salt) per serving?
6. Which package contains eight servings?
7. Which contain the preservative, BHA?
8. Which has the most grams of fat per serving?
9. Which label says the contents have 120 calories in one tablespoon?

Answers: 1. 4;   2. 5, 7;   3. 3;   4. 1, 3, 4, 5, 6, 7;   5. 6;   6. 1;   7. 1, 7;   8. 2;   9. 2

It doesn't take long. Take a deep breath and begin moving.

CHAPTER 7

A Little Exercise, Please

First of all, before we write about a warm-up exercise program, there are some things you must understand about exercise. Exercises must be repeated several times, and at a rate that speeds up your breathing and heart beat. Exact information about how fast your heart should beat depends on each individual. However, here's a rule of thumb:

An exercise program should be hard enough to get you to sweat a little across the forehead, and should be kept up for fifteen to thirty minutes, each time. The set of exercises should be repeated at least three times a week to make any progress—five times is best. After you reach your goal weight, twice-a-week exercise is a minimum for maintaining fitness.

We're going to call the exercises that follow our Double Duty Dozen—3D, for short—because they strengthen your muscles, improve your breathing, and tone up your body. Do them in the order suggested so that you warm up your muscles and get fresh blood flowing into them before giving them a brisk workout.

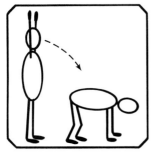

1. REACH UP, REACH DOWN—
Stand with feet as wide apart as
your shoulders. Raise straight
arms high overhead. Reach high
and stretch your middle. Feel
the pull. Then bend to touch
your toes. Go down as far as you
can with straight legs, then
bend your knees if you must, to touch the floor and feel
the backs of your legs stretch. Begin with eight and work
up to sixteen reaches.

2. LION STRETCH—Keeping
both your feet on the floor, and
knees slightly bent, bend over
and walk your hands ahead
about three feet, or whatever is
comfortable for your size. With
your head down, arch your back
up, the way you see a dog, cat,
or a lion stretch when it wakes up. Now drop your seat
toward the floor. Stretch the muscles on the opposite
side of your trunk. Move slowly. You will feel the stretch
deep in your legs and body. Begin with eight stretches,
up and down, and work up to twelve. Remember, don't
do these quickly, and don't jerk your back.

3. ROCKING HORSE—Lay on the floor, face down. Grab your ankles behind you. Rock slowly back and forth on your stomach eight times. Work up to twelve.

4. DOUGHNUT CURLS—Roll over on your back. Bend your knees and keep them slightly apart, with your feet flat on the floor. With hands behind your head, let your stomach muscles pull you up so your elbows touch your knees. Do this eight times. This collapses the "doughnut" circling your middle.

5. MOTOCROSS—Lay on your back with your hands palms down under your hips. Lift your legs and begin pedaling a make-believe bicycle in the air. Go fast enough to win the race. Do 25 strokes, counting each push with the right foot as one stroke. Work for increased speed, rather than more strokes.

6. JUMPING JACK AND JILLS—Begin in a standing position. Clap your hands over your head and jump your feet apart at the same time. Jump back to the standing position. Begin with eight of these. Depending on your weight, you may be uncomfortable with these at first. Work up to 25.

7. OLYMPIC—While still standing, reach in front of you, and pretend to be swimming the overhand crawl stroke. Pull against the make-believe water. Move your head sideways to breathe, just as if you were in the pool. Begin with eight and work up to 32 strokes with each arm. Be sure to keep your breathing deep and steady, just like an Olympic swimmer.

8. DISAPPEARING STOMACH—
Standing, put your hands on
your knees and force all the air
out of your lungs. Now pull
your stomach in tight, for the
count of three, then breathe in
and push your stomach out. Do
eight of these to deepen your

breathing and tighten your stomach muscles. This also
brings extra blood to the inside of your abdomen, tuning
up the organs that digest your food.

9. LONG-DISTANCE HIKE—
Begin walking around the inside of your house. Climb the
stairs, if you have some. Circle
the table, if you can (but don't
stop in the kitchen). Walk all
around, down the hall and out
the door. Outside, walk around

trees, bushes, cars and bikes in the driveway, or any other
object, even the garbage can. Keep walking, and sing a
good walking song to yourself (or out loud if it doesn't
bother anyone!) Walk to the beat of your song and think
of songs with faster beats on following days. Walk 15
minutes.

10. SHARED EXERCISE—Now you are warmed up for a good romp with the dog, a session of jump rope, dribbling the basketball, riding your bicycle, or taking a spin on the skateboard. You'll think of something. With all that oxygen filling new places in your lungs, and the power of energized muscles, you'll be able to continue your activities for hours. Your body will continue to burn calories at a faster rate, even if you go back to sitting.

11. WARM DOWN—Pull a few weeds, empty the garbage, clean the bathroom sink. Take five minutes to help with the chores.

12. EXHALING THE FAT—Sit in a chair and breathe in deeply, to the bottom of the muscles you are sitting on; then blow out all the burned-up energy. Clear your lungs completely, but don't get dizzy. Think about the hundreds of cells of fat you've  emptied with your workout, and how you've reduced the supply of stored energy.

Studies show that normal-weight people exercise more than fat people, and play with more energy at their games.

Remember, you've changed your image to that of a normal-weight person, and you have to do the things a normal-weight person would do.

You'll begin to notice improvements in your muscles in a few days, and in your appearance in a few weeks.

It doesn't take long. Take a deep breath and begin moving.

*Do it a day at a time. You can,
you know!*

CHAPTER 8

A Plan for Action

In this chapter we are going to talk more about what YOU can do to help YOURSELF.

An easy way to begin is with a record. Get a small notebook, or fold some blank papers into pocket-size pieces. On this paper you are going to write down the things that you think are causing you to overeat, and we will remind you of ways to solve these issues. In the end, the hard work of changing will fall to you, but maybe we can help with ideas.

• *Do you overeat to get your parents to notice you?*

If you would like more attention from your Mother or Dad, you might try asking for it, instead of starting a war over your eating habits. Say, "Dad, could we do something together?" or, "Mom, can I sit and talk to you?" Just as little birds learn to fly, gather seeds, and build nests from their big parent birds, so children learn to be like adult men and women by being around them and doing things with them. Parents help their children learn to explore the world and live usefully in it.

If you answer yes to this question, write in your notebook:

       1. Attention from my parents.

- *Do you overeat because you're angry?*

Learn to talk about your feelings when you are angry. Say, "I'm mad about that. That makes me angry." You can say this without having a tantrum. People will believe you.

We know of a person who felt really angry one day. He went to the candy store and spent his whole allowance on chocolate bars. After eating them, he still felt angry. Then he decided to go into the bathroom and yell really loudly. He found that that made him feel better. He got his "mad" out of the way without punishing himself with an eating binge.

Now sometimes you have to tackle a problem head on. Go to the person and say in a pleasant voice, if you can, "I want to talk to you about a situation that is making me angry." Then state the situation. If that person begins shouting at you, walk away. Do not get involved in a shouting match. Wait until things calm down, then try again. Sometimes a person will refuse to talk about a solution to the problem. You may have to beat a pillow to get rid of your anger and frustration. Don't go to the refrigerator for a sandwich. It doesn't help.

If you eat because you're angry, write in your notebook:

2. To calm my anger.

• *Do you eat because you're lonely?*

Think of something you could do besides eat when you are alone. Maybe you could go see a friend or call someone on the phone. Read a book. Take a walk. Draw a picture. Go swimming. Whatever you do, stay away from the kitchen. Make a list of activities on a separate piece of paper and tape it to your closet door. When you feel lonely, go look at this list. It may be a good time to work on unfinished projects that are sitting at the bottom of your closet.

If you eat because you're lonely, write in your notebook:

3. When I'm lonely.

• *Do you eat when you have nothing to do?*

Give your hands a task that feels good and puts your head to work, too. Learn to knit a simple sweater, or grow a flower garden. Play records, work a crossword puzzle. Begin making handicrafts for people you'll be giving presents to. Ask your parents for ideas of things you could do for them.

If you eat because you have nothing to do, write:

4. Nothing else to do.

• *Do you eat because you see food on the counter?*

Ask your parents not to buy snack foods that tempt you. If they like to eat these things, ask them to keep their snacks out of sight when you are around. Prepare some bite-size vegetable snacks to have handy when you feel an attack of munchies coming on. Most of the time, it will be best to stay out of the kitchen, away from the counter, and across the room from the popcorn bowl.

If you eat because you see food, write on your paper:

5. The sight of food.

• *Do you eat because you are depressed about the way you look?*

We all need help when it comes to making changes. Old habits don't like to be disturbed. You will be able to make yourself look better, but it will not happen overnight, or even this week. Every extra pound went on your body one at a time, and it will come off just as slowly.

It means you have to stick with your plan, but you can do it. Say to yourself, "I'm just as smart and as tough as other people who have lost weight. If other people can do it, so can I. I'm not going to feel depressed about this. I'm working on improvements, and that makes me feel good. I'm changing my eating habits."

If you eat because you feel depressed about your appearance, write:

6. I don't like the way I look.

Keep your notebook handy. You will think of other things to write in it. You may even want to note your progress. On many days you'll be able to write:

Today, I ate all the recommended servings of foods in the food groups, and I skipped those on the junk food chart. I'm making progress changing my eating habits.

Do it a day at a time. You can, you know!

*From now on expect small amounts
of improvement every day.*

CHAPTER 9

Working Toward Your Goal

In this chapter we are going to suggest ways to work at your goal of changing your overeating habits. First, review the things you've read so far:

You've performed the mirror test and checked the weight chart. That gave you a pretty good idea of the weight that is normal for someone your height and age. Self-esteem and taking charge were shown to be necessary in overcoming overeating. You've learned how to begin to deal with other people's attitudes about being overweight. You've asked for the help of your family and other trusted adults. You've learned how to select nutritious food in servings appropriate for your needs. Exercise is becoming part of your life. You've made a list of reasons you overeat.

Following are some goals that you can work toward. You may want to add some of these ideas to your notebook. You are not going to worry about pounds and inches; those will take care of themselves when your eating habits come under your control. These goals involve things you can do besides eating, and ways you can slow down your eating.

Set regular times and places where you can eat and enjoy your food.

A good place would be the kitchen or dining room table. Make a rule for yourself that you will only eat when you are sitting at the table, even if you're eating an after-school snack of fruit.

People who eat in the family room while they watch television, on the porch while they talk to Dad or Mom, or while talking on the phone eat more food, because they eat without thinking about it. They also begin to think that every time they are in front of the television set they must eat. All of a sudden, eating and being on the porch seem to go together, or eating and being on the phone.

GOAL: *From now on, you will only eat while sitting at the table.*

Arrange your food attractively on your plate.

Cut your radishes into rose forms if that pleases you. Put your salad in a special bowl, if that makes it look more appealing. Stir everything together into a hash mountain if that looks good to you. Have food that makes your mouth water, just seeing it there on the plate.

GOAL: *From now on, you will take time to arrange your food in a pleasing manner.*

Eat slowly.

It takes about fifteen minutes for your brain to signal that your stomach is full. Give it time. Otherwise, you will be too full before you know it. Overweight people usually eat too fast, and they eat more food than anyone else at the table in the same time.

GOAL: *From now on, you will take one bite of food and chew and swallow it before you take another bite.*

Decide what foods you will eat yourself.

Do not let the television commercials or the clock or your school chums talk you into eating cream-filled cakes—unless that's what you really want. You must be prepared to sit at the table and eat the cakes slowly from a pretty cake plate, and to think about eating.

GOAL: *From now on, you will be in charge of every bite of food you put in your mouth.*

Find a buddy who wants to help you, and stay away from friends who tease you into eating more than you want.

The buddy system will help you keep your mind off food. It works like this: Find a friend who wants to begin an eating control program, too. Then stick together. When name callers hurt your feelings, you can encourage each other. You can help each other walk past the candy store without stopping. You can call your buddy when you feel like eating. Talk about things other than food.

GOAL: *From now on, you will ask your friends to be buddies in your overeating control program.*

Learn to listen to other people.

Get your mind off food and what you weigh, and explore the ideas of others. Talk to others and really listen to what they say. If you can put food out of your mind, it will not have so firm a grip on you.

GOAL: *From now on, you will explore the world of other people's ideas. You do not have time to think about food.*

Have a supply of low-calorie munchies on hand.

These can be from this book's food chart.

Six Super Salads

Golden Carrot Wonder—Wash and shred two un-unpeeled carrots. Add a tablespoon of frozen or fresh orange juice. Stir and eat.

Hawaiian Cabbage—Shred one-fourth head of fresh cabbage. Sprinkle with dried onion bits. Add enough pineapple juice to make moist but not soupy. Stir. Let the salad sit for about 15 minutes, then eat.

Waldorf Salad—Chop one unpeeled red-skinned apple (leave out the core!), two stalks of celery, and a dozen walnut halves. Add 1/4 cup of pine-apple juice. Stir and let sit ten minutes. Eat.

Apple Flutter—Make one packet of unflavored, un-sweetened gelatin according to package direc-tions, then stir in one cup of applesauce. Place in refrigerator until set. Top with a spoonful of yogurt.

Red and Green Salad—Chop one garden-fresh to-mato and two green onions into a bowl. Add 1-1/2 cups of cooked fresh green beans or a can of drained green beans. Add one tablespoon of mayonnaise, one tablespoon of lemon juice, and a pinch of dill weed or salad herbs. Toss. Chill fifteen minutes. Serve.

Celebration Cantaloupe—Scoop the seeds from half a small cantaloupe. Fill center with a heap of cottage cheese. Add six washed strawberries. Serve.

Keep these in the kitchen. Never allow food to be in your room, because that's the place where you will be most likely to eat without thinking.

GOAL: *From now on, if you get a strong urge to eat something, you will have acceptable food handy. You will eat these munchies at the table, too.*

Drink several glasses of water every day.

Have a tall glass of tap water when you feel empty. Every boy and girl should drink six glasses of water every day. Water won't cause you to gain weight, unlike soda and other sweetened drinks. Your body cells are mostly water, and you need a steady supply to replace the water lost when you go to the bathroom or sweat.

GOAL: *From now on, you will drink clear fresh water when you feel thirsty, and avoid sugary sodas.*

Learn to say no to extra helpings.

Before you add more food to your plate, ask yourself if you really need this food. Are you eating it because it's there and you like the taste?

GOAL: *From now on, you will eat smaller amounts of foods you like.*

Always eat breakfast.

You'll be too hungry to make it to lunch without breakfast. When the first snack comes into sight, you'll grab it and eat twice as much as you would have at breakfast. Like anything else on the go, bodies need fuel to get started in the the mornings.

GOAL: *From now on, you will eat a breakfast made up of foods in the allowed food groups in the right amounts.*

Forget about crash diets.

We mean diets with unusual food combinations (eggs and grapefruit), or starvation rations (one meal a day). These do not provide any long-term weight loss. When you gain the pounds back that you starved off, you'll be more depressed than ever.

GOAL: *From now on, you will eat regular meals at mealtimes and will select nutritious foods from many food groups.*

Get lots of exercise.

Get out of the chair, away from the TV and video, and away from the kitchen. Run, jump, and do active things. Just cutting back on food isn't the whole answer. Exercise. Fat hates to be disturbed. For ideas, refer back to the chapter on exercise.

GOAL: *From now on, you will find active things to do for at least thirty minutes every day.*

Be honest with yourself and set goals you can reach.

Do not think you will lose a big amount overnight. If you expect to be able to lose your extra pounds quickly, you are setting yourself up for a big letdown. That will be hard on your new eating control plan.

GOAL: *From now on, expect small amounts of improvement every day.*

Believe in yourself, and believe that you can control your eating habits.

Old habits change slowly, but you CAN change them. You'll need encouragement. Ask your parents for help and words of praise. Talk about things besides food. Tell them, "It makes me feel good when you tell me you love me, or that I did a good job cleaning my room, or that my body is looking more attractive because I've changed my ways of eating."

Everyone in your family will feel better when food is no longer the only issue talked about.
GOAL: *From now on, you will feel your self-esteem growing because you have learned to handle a really difficult problem in your life.*

Now, before we close this chapter, let's say something about telling you, "From now on you will. . ." do this or that behavior. We are not ordering you to change. You have to do that yourself. You are the only one who can change you, and most likely you can change only yourself.

By telling you what you CAN do, we hope you will take hold of the habit of overeating and change it yourself. We're rooting for you, through all the ups and downs, until you reach your goal.

*You are not the only one who has to have
an eating control program.*

CHAPTER 10

Extra Help

Many scientific studies about food, nutrition, weight control, eating patterns, self-esteem, over-eating control, and diets are being performed by doctors and scientists all over the country. Being overweight or underweight is a problem for at least half of the population, young or old, male or female. You are not the only one who has to have an eating control program; however, each person must work out his or her own solution.

In preparing the material for this book, we read some very helpful information in the books listed later. The best way for you to find good reading material is to ask the school librarian or a librarian at the public library. The books we mention may not be on the shelves where you get your books. New books are being printed every season with the latest information about food and diet. Magazines feature articles with ideas about weight control. There is much material available, and you will have to decide which is most helpful to you.

Jane Brody's Nutrition Book (W.W. Norton and

Co., 1981), says it's *A Lifetime Guide to Good Eating for Better Health and Weight Control,* and indeed it seemed to us to be easy to use and to cover many questions. The chapter on "Child Feeding in the Junk-Food Generation" has some excellent information, aimed mostly at adults. If you're not turned off by big books, you could learn a lot from this book, too. There is also an interesting chapter on reading food labels.

Know Your Nutrition: The Complete Guide to Good Health Through Natural Living by Linda Clark (Keats Publishing, 1973) is a smaller, paperbound book, with just about everything you ever wanted to know about vitamins and minerals. We bought our copy at a health food store.

The Diet Center Program: Lose Weight Fast and Keep it Off Forever, by Sybil Ferguson (Little, Brown, 1983) has some good chapters on setting goals and becoming your own nutritionist. At the back of this book are about thirty pages of food charts to help you select foods according to fats, carbohydrates, protein, and water content.

Pillsbury's Family Weight Control Cookbook: Menus and Recipes Low in Calories and High in Nutrition (Pillsbury Publications, 1970) has some especially good low-calorie recipes.

Seven Ways to Keep from Losing Weight

Blame your Mom, Tom.

Wait 'til next week, Deke.

Grab a snack, Jack.

Just one won't hurt, Bert.

Clean your plate, Kate.

Watch the TV, Stevie.

Don't make a choice, Joyce.

Seven Ways to Keep from Gaining Weight

Jump rope, Hope.

Ride your bike, Mike.

Climb the stair, Clare.

Throw the ball, Paul.

Skip the dip, Chip.

Have the toast plain, Jane.

Pass up the jelly, Kelly.

Metropolitan Life's Four Steps To Weight Control, published by Metropolitan Life Insurance Company in 1969, is an easy-to-read guide with food charts, suggested diets, reasons to lose extra pounds, and suggestions for a lunch-box meal. You might be able to get a copy by calling the local office of this insurance company. Life insurance companies are experts on what makes people live longer, and generally that has to do with good diet and normal weight.

Slim Forever: the Diet Control Center's Diet by Mary Sargent (Bantam Books, 1975) has a chapter on good beginnings for children. This book has nice ideas about how to change your thinking about the foods you eat. The last half of the book is recipes for low-calorie cooking.

Finally, *The You Can Do It! Kids Diet* by Dee Matthews (Holt, Rinehart and Winston, 1985) and *Fat Free: Common Sense for Young Weight Worriers* by Sara Gilbert (Macmillan, 1975) are books written especially for young people.

This list is just a sample. We think once you start learning about foods and their value to your body (or lack of value, in some cases), you'll want to continue. It's interesting to learn something that will help you the rest of your life.

We wish you good health!

APPENDIX A

Learning to Shop

Because you are learning to take charge when it comes to eating, you may want to know about getting good foods when you go to the store. First, we've listed some fruits and vegetables and have given tips on picking out the best of fresh foods. Then we've given some advice on what to look for at the meat counter, in the dairy case, and on the shelf.

The Produce Department

Many people don't know how to recognize good items in the fresh produce section of their grocery. Here's what we've learned over the years.

Grapes—Look for green stems and plump, firm grapes. After washing the grapes, store in the refrigerator. They'll keep at least a week. Try freezing some seedless grapes for a snack.

Oranges—Look for smooth skins, free from spots and

soft areas. The fruit should feel firm and heavy. They will last two to three weeks stored in a refrigerator.

Bananas—To be fully ripe, a banana should have brown spots on the outside of its skin. These are called sugar spots. A banana will not ripen as it should in a refrigerator; however, once it is ripe (covered with sugar spots) it will keep longer in the refrigerator. Green bananas will ripen in three or four days. Overripe bananas make good milkshakes when put in the blender with lowfat milk.

Apples—There are several thousand varieties of apples, but you are likely to have a selection of only six or eight in your supermarket. Apples are available all year, so decide which variety you like best, and keep a supply on hand. Choose firm, smooth-skinned fruit that doesn't look wilted or wrinkled. Check the ends for worm holes, if you buy your apples at a roadside stand. Apples will keep for weeks.

Tomatoes—Choose firm, rosy red tomatoes. Paler tomatoes will ripen on the back of your counter, but the best flavor comes from those ripened, or nearly ripened, on the vine. Avoid soft or mushy tomatoes, or ones that have black spots on the skin. Tomatoes are best eaten as fresh as possible; don't buy more than you can eat in a week.

Cucumbers—Choose straight cucumbers that are not too big around. Fat cukes have large seeds inside that may be unpleasant to eat. Skins should be deep green and full-looking, not wrinkled. Store in the refrigerator, and eat in a week to ten days.

Lettuce—Head lettuce is the most popular kind and keeps longer than leaf lettuce. Look for medium-soft heads that feel springy when you squeeze them gently and have a nice green color. Mostly white-looking lettuce, and too-firm heads, mean the lettuce was left on the plant too long and has become old and bitter. It turns brown or becomes slimy if kept too long. Store in refrigerator and eat in a week.

Potatoes—There are several kinds, with different flavors and textures. Do not buy potatoes that have started to sprout, or are turning green along the skin. Store in a cool place and cook in nature's package, the skin. Uncooked, they should keep six to eight weeks.

Apricots—These are one of the few fruits you will want to buy and eat when they are soft. Choose those with a golden-yellow color. Wash and eat them. They do not keep well. Buy only as many as you can eat in three days.

Green beans—Look for bright green, fresh, young beans.

Old, dark-colored ones are likely to be tough and strong tasting. Beans are best when eaten the same day they are picked. If you buy yours at the market, eat them as soon as possible.

Corn on the cob—Select ears that have fresh green-colored outside leaves, and pale yellow kernels inside, on the cob. Pull a bit of the top leaves back to see the kernels inside, and to make sure there are no "critters" munching on the tasty ears. Cook the corn as soon as possible. Every day it is off the plant it becomes tougher.

Cherries—Look for shiny deep red or black skins to get the sweetest. Avoid mushy or moldy looking fruit. The best way to eat cherries is to wash them when you get them home from the store and eat them that day. It's better to buy a pound and eat cherries with your family every day than to buy ten pounds and stuff yourself all on one afternoon. Cherries have a way of letting you know that's a big mistake—with a stomachache!

Plums—Be sure your plums look and smell fresh when you buy them, and have firm (not damaged, wrinkled, or sticky) skins. Plums will not keep very long. Buy only what you can eat in a few days. Storing them in the refrigerator will keep them fresh a day or two.

Cauliflower—Heads of cauliflower should be white and compact. Check the leaves at the base to be sure they are not wilted or discolored. The flowerets should not be spotted brown: that means the cauliflower is old, tough, and possibly bitter tasting.

Carrots—Buy bright orange, straight, long, slim carrots, with the leaves attached if possible. When the tops are clipped, it is hard to know if the carrots are old. Old carrots taste woody and a little bitter. This vegetable is available all year around, and keeps weeks in the refrigerator. Keep some handy for a snack.

These are just a few of the fruits and vegetables offered in your market. Look over the selection and ask the people who work in the produce section about buying and using the items there. Some markets have free folders for customers giving nutritional information, recipes, and storage suggestions.

The Meat Counter

Here are some tips on selecting fresh meat, poultry, and fish.

Chicken—When selecting chicken, look for skin that is moist and not heavily wrinkled. Buy frying rather than stewing chickens—they have less fat. When you cook and eat your chicken, remove the skin; that's where most of the chicken fat is. Chicken is an excellent food.

Turkey—Again, look for plump, moist skin. Avoid turkey (or chicken) that has a strong smell. Many stores sell turkey parts now, so that you don't have to buy a whole bird. Turkey, like chicken, is low in fat and full of nutrition. Bake it in foil or grill it slowly on a barbecue; you can brush it with a little vegetable oil and add a sprinkle of garlic powder or onion powder for extra flavor. Remove the skin before eating.

Beef—Ask the butcher to help you find the very leanest beef. There are usually several kinds of ground beef (hamburger) at the meat counter; look for the package that shows the lowest percentage of fat or that says "extra lean" on it. Ask the butcher's help in picking out other cuts of lean beef—there are many to choose from. When you cook a hamburger, try broiling it or grilling it instead of frying it. That way, extra fat will drip off the meat.

Fish—Fresh fish should feel firm and compact and have either a pleasant "fishy" smell or no smell. Do not buy fish with a heavy, unpleasant odor. When you cook fish, try sealing it in a pouch of foil and baking it. Beforehand, brush it with a little vegetable oil and add a sprinkle of dill or oregano. Squeeze a little fresh lemon on it for extra zip. (If you buy frozen fish, get a kind that has no coating on it.)

Lunch meats—In general, we'd advise you to use cold sliced turkey, chicken, or beef for your sandwiches. Most lunch meats have large amounts of fat and salt in them, and should be eaten only once in a great while. Many kinds of bologna, salami, ham, and other lunch meats are in this category. Try to think of new sandwiches and combinations—an all-vegetable sandwich or a peanut-butter-and-banana combo can be delicious.

Remember, all fresh meats, including chicken, turkey, beef, and fish, must be kept in the refrigerator until time to prepare them for eating. Left at room temperature, these foods will spoil in less than half a day, and may be unsafe to eat after only a few hours. Do not risk making yourself sick by handling your meat carelessly.

Even in the refrigerator, meats will keep only a short time if not cooked. Buy no more fresh meat than you can use in three days. Cooked meats will usually keep five days if they are kept cold.

Some other products:

Dairy products—Look for the word "lowfat" or a very
low percentage of fat on packages. Buy skim milk
and lowfat yogurt and cheeses. Try to eat as little
as possible of high-fat cheeses such as cheddar,
Swiss, gouda, and cream cheeses. Ice cream is also very high in fat, and should only be eaten
on special occasions.

In large markets, dairy products are dated on the
container. Learn where to find the date and how to
read it. Then be sure to buy only the freshest products
in the case.

Milk, butter, most cheeses, and margarine have
dates that tell customers when a food has reached
the limit of freshness. Cereals, mayonnaise, peanut
butter, jams, crackers, and an increasing number of
other food items on the grocers' shelves are stamped
by the manufacturer, "Sell by (month and year)."
Use this as a guide to select the freshest items.

Certainly, you will never want to purchase food
whose calendar sell-date has already passed.

Breads, grains, and pastas—These foods should be
included in the foods you eat every day, but not in
big amounts. Try whole grain breads and cereals (un-
sweetened), whole-wheat or soy pasta, and brown

rice—they're all very tasty. Stay away from canned spaghetti and macaroni. There are usually lots of hidden calories and fat in the meats and sauces included in the can.

Store cereals in dry places. Little critters, such as weevils and moths, like to build their homes in full cereal boxes. If you should get home with a cereal box that has ingredients crawling out to greet you, return it to the grocer for replacement. Never put it in your cupboard. Eat your cereals, pastas, and rice while they are fresh. The quality of nutrients is best in fresh foods.

APPENDIX B

What Does a Vitamin Do for You?

Vitamin A: Necessary for good growth in children and good health in adults. Especially important for good vision and healthy skin. Helps your body keep the linings of your nose, mouth, and and other body openings in good repair.

Best sources: liver, cantaloupe, sweet potatoes, spinach, broccoli, carrots, apricots, tomatoes, egg yolk, milk products.

Vitamin B complex: The B vitamins are often known by their chemical names:

Thiamine (B_1): Encourages growth, healthy nerves, and good digestion.

Best sources: dried peas and beans, liver, fish, poultry, eggs, milk, whole grain breads, cereal.

Riboflavin (B_2): Necessary for digestion and growth, it also helps the body turn fats, carbohydrates, and proteins into available energy.

Best sources: yeast, peanuts, whole wheat flour, liver, kidney, heart.

Niacin (B$_3$): Important for healthy skin and nerves; helps prevent nervousness, depression, and problems in the intestines.

Best sources: fish, lean meat, poultry, whole grain breads, cereals, flour, white potatoes, peanuts, almonds, eggs.

Pantothenic Acid: Helps turn food into usable energy.

Best sources: lean meat, whole grain cereal and bread, egg yolks, peanuts, almonds, walnuts.

Biotin: Helps your veins, arteries, and skin stay healthy, and aids in digesting food.

Best sources: liver, eggs, nuts, many vegetables, brown rice.

Pyridoxine (B$_6$): Keeps teeth and gums, blood cells, and nerves healthy.

Best sources: fish, whole-grain foods, meat, poultry, yeast, many vegetables.

Folic Acid: Helps produce red blood cells and prevents anemia, a blood disorder.

Best sources: spinach, cauliflower, broccoli, lean meat, poultry, fish, yeast.

Vitamin B₁₂: Helps the body form red blood cells, and aids the nervous system in functioning.

Best sources: liver, eggs, lean meats, milk products.

Vitamin C: Needed by every tissue in the body, because it helps grow and maintain your teeth, bones, and blood, and aids wounds in healing. This vitamin can't be stored in the body; every day you must get a new supply.

Best sources: oranges, grapefruit, strawberries, cabbage, cauliflower, potatoes, tomatoes, green pepper.

Vitamin D: Needed by the body to make use of calcium in building strong teeth and bones.

Best sources: sunshine (!) Sometimes Vitamin D is added to milk, where it works with the calcium.

Vitamin E: Important to good skin because it helps cell membranes stay healthy

Best sources: wheat germ, whole-grain foods, many vegetable oils

Vitamin K: Essential to the blood's ability to clot

Best sources: spinach, cauliflower, broccoli, cabbage, liver.

GLOSSARY

addiction (uh·DIHK·shuhn)—a very strong mental or physical need for something, like drugs, alcohol, gambling, or food

artery (AR·tuh·ree)—in the body, a type of major blood vessel that carries blood from the heart to various body parts

artificial (ar·tuh·FIHSH·uhl)—made or manufactured by humans; not from nature

attitude (AT·uh·tood)—how a person feels toward a fact (like war) or a state (like being overweight)

binge (BIHNJ)—to act in an out-of-control manner, especially in eating and drinking

calorie (KAL·uh·ree)—a small unit of food that produces energy for the body

carbohydrate (kar·boh·HY·drayt)—a major class of of food nutrients. Foods with sugars, starches, and/or cellulose are in this class

circulatory system/circulation (SER·kyoo·luh·toh·ree SIHS·tuhm/ser·kyoo·LAY·shuhn)—the *circulatory system* (arteries, veins, capillaries, heart, and lymph system) keeps blood flowing throughout the body. This flow of blood is the *circulation*

counselor (KOWN·seh·ler)—a person whose job is to give advice that helps others understand problems and find solutions for them

criticize/criticism/critical (KRIHT·uh·syz/KRIHT·uh·syzuhm/KRIHT·ih·kuhl)—to *criticize* is to judge someone or something and then point out faults. *Criticism* is that judgment; someone who points out faults is being *critical*

digestive system/digestion (dy·JES·tihv SIHS·tuhm/dy·JES·chun)—the *digestive system* (the mouth and salivary glands, esophagus, liver, gall bladder, stomach, pancreas, intestines, and rectum) breaks down food into particles usable to the body, sends those particles to the bloodstream, and gets rid of food bits that cannot be used. *Digestion* is the process of breaking down food

fiber (FY·ber)—in a diet, coarse food that is not digested by the body, but that helps food move along through the digestive system

frustration (fruhs·TRAY·shuhn)—a feeling as if nothing you can do or say will ever change a bad situation or cause anything at all to happen

heredity (huh·RED·ih·tee)—qualities in a person that come either from genes or from family traditions

ingredient (ihn·GREE·dee·ent)—one of the parts in a mixture or combination of things

jealous/jealousy (JEL·uhs/JEL·uh·see)—to be *jealous* is to resent someone because he or she has qualities or things that you don't think you have. *Jealousy* is this feeling of resentment

membranes (MEM·braynz)—thin layers, as in body cells, that hold those cells together and separate them from other cells

minerals (MIHN·uh·ruhls)—in a diet, substances (like calcium, potassium, or zinc) that occur in food which are needed by the body's cells and organs

nutrient (NOO·tree·ent)—chemical substances, gotten from food, that help build and repair body cells, give bodies energy, and keep the body running correctly. The five nutrients are vitamins, minerals, protein, carbohydrates, and fats

nutritious/nutrition (noo·TRIH·shuhs/noo·TRIH· shuhn)—diets that are *nutritious* give people the right amount of nutrients to grow and function well. *Nutrition* is the science of good food and how that food is used by the body

overeating (oh·ver·EET·ing)—to eat more food than your body can use

preservative (pree·ZERV·uh·tihv)—something added to food to stop natural processes such as rotting or changing color

professional (proh·FESH·uh·nuhl)—here, a professional is a person whose job it is to help people look at and change certain thoughts, feelings, and behaviors that cause problems for those people. These might be a counselor, psychologist, psychiatrist, nurse, social worker, or other mental health worker

protein (PROH·teen)—in a diet, protein foods (meat, poultry, eggs, dried peas and beans, milk and milk products) are one of the major food groups. They help build, maintain, and repair body cells and keep body systems functioning

recreation (rek·ree·AY·shuhn)—activities that are fun and that help people relax

self-esteem (SELF es·TEEM)—how a person feels about himself or herself and what he or she does

spoilage retardant (SPOYL·ihj ree·TAHR·dent)— something added to foods to keep them from spoiling or rotting

stabilizer (STAY·bih·ly·zer)—something added to foods to keep them looking exactly as they did when they left the food plant

vitamin (VY·tuh·mihn)—chemical substances nec- essary to good nutrition and to the functioning of the body. Vitamins are known by letters (Vita- min C, Vitamin E) or by their chemical names (niacin, riboflavin)

INDEX

About the Authors

Gail Jones Sanchez, a licensed clinical social worker, has been counseling adults, teens, and children with overeating problems since 1978. She was inspired to write *Overeating* because she saw a need for material that "validates that an overweight child has more to deal with than just food. This book is about self-discovery; it explores *why* a person overeats."

Ms. Sanchez is the coauthor of *Let's Talk About Sex and Loving,* a book on sex education for parents and children. She lectures and gives workshops on both sex education and overeating in addition to her private practice in Milpitas, California.

Mary Gerbino, a freelance writer, also understands how difficult it can be to change overeating habits. "I dealt with my own overeating habit and those of my two sons," she says. "I know it takes patience, understanding, and a great deal of sharing, but it can be done!"

Ms. Gerbino has published many articles in newspapers and magazines and was a columnist for the *San Jose Sun.* She is coauthor of both *Let's Talk About Sex and Loving* and *You Deserve It: A Guide for Women* (retitled *La Vida En Careja*). In addition to giving piano lessons, she has taught children's religious education classes for ten years.